Nicholas Hawksmoor
London Churches

Size 2
NA
5497
.H39
A4
2015

Nicholas Hawksmoor

London Churches

Mohsen Mostafavi
Hélène Binet

Lars Müller Publishers

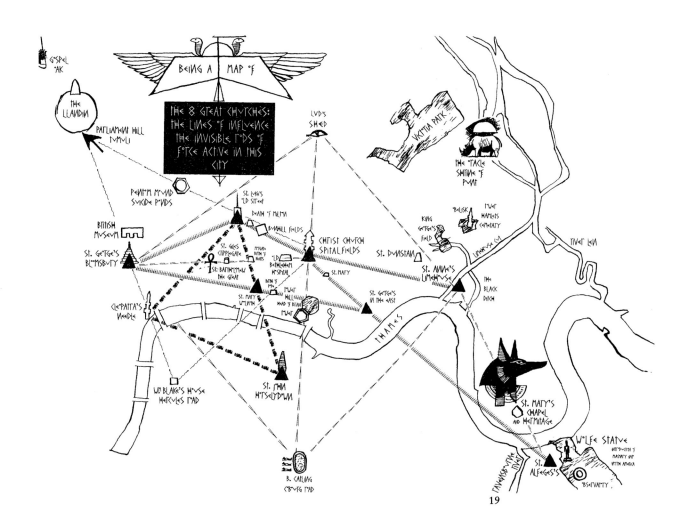

Map of Hawksmoor's London churches, showing 'lines of influence and invisible rods of force'
between the churches and the city of London.

Methodical Imaginings
Nicholas Hawksmoor's London Churches

Mohsen Mostafavi

Nicholas Hawksmoor (c. 1661–1736) figures large in the imagination of architects and of architecture. He was an important part of his own generation and worked closely with the leading architects of his day, including Wren and Vanbrugh. He is often referred to as a Baroque architect who suffered the consequences of the shift in tastes, during his own lifetime, towards the more formal simplicity and purity of Palladianism. Overtaken by the demands of a new era, Hawksmoor became a half-forgotten architect whose renaissance and rediscovery as an exemplary architect of his day has as much to do with fiction as with fact.

'And so let us beginne; and, as the Fabrick takes its Shape in front of you, always keep the Structure intirely in Mind as you inscribe it. First, you must measure out or cast the Area in as exact a Manner as can be, and then you must draw the Plot and make the Scale. I have imparted to you the Principles of Terrour and Magnificence, for these you must represent in the due placing of Parts and Ornaments as well as in the Proportions of the several Orders: you see, Walter, how I take my Pen?'

So begins Peter Ackroyd's dark and masterful narration in *Hawksmoor,* a book that did much to help articulate the architectural qualities and enhance the reputation of the real Hawksmoor – even though Ackroyd makes his architect an occultist. The fictional character's wish for architecture to impart both 'Terrour' and 'Magnificence' through the juxtaposition of the parts, ornaments and proportions is a brilliant and concise description of the non-fictional architect's intentions, a sense of awe and bewilderment being one of the key characteristics of his work.

The scope of Hawksmoor's work extends from institutional buildings and hospitals to universities and country houses. But no single project better describes his position in relation to its time than a collection of churches he designed following an Act of Parliament of 1711 for the building of fifty new churches in

London and Westminster. The Act brought together religious, social and political interests and aimed to make the idea of a new age visible by building on open sites in the expanding eastern part of the city. While a large number of churches had been built under the supervision of Wren following the Great Fire of 1666, these churches were often on old infill sites and not always seen from a distance. By contrast, the Act of 1711 conceived of the new churches as a key component of the urban development process.

A commission including Wren and Vanbrugh appointed Hawksmoor and William Dickinson as surveyors. The two were essentially put in charge of the supervision of the overall project, finding and measuring sites and making sure that the works were properly executed. Political upheaval soon put an end to the ambitious aspirations of the Act, and only a dozen of the churches were completed. Nevertheless, it is the churches built by Hawksmoor that best exemplify the intentions of the Act, while also representing the most coherent manifestation of Hawksmoor's own architectural ideas.

The building of the new churches was in many respects a collaborative process that involved the cross-fertilisation and communication of multiple ideas and agendas – from religious to architectural. Architects not only worked individually, but also together, and were even asked to contribute to improving each other's work. At one point the commission seems to have recommended the concept of a single design or form as a general direction for the building of all the churches. Vanbrugh stressed the importance of 'Solemn and Awfull Appearance both within and without'. These discussions and recommendations point to the importance of the churches as an ensemble – a totality – representing less the significance of an individual building and more the consequences of the whole. The interrelationship between the intentions of the clergy and the ideas of architects points towards the desire for the formation of a syncretic vision of the Anglican church, with its roots in a more 'primitive' notion of Christianity.

In general Hawksmoor seems to have reserved solemnity for the interior of his churches, as the appropriate setting for religious ritual. These are invariably axial and planar, and refer to earlier, 'ancient' traditions of building. And the outside is where Hawksmoor, through a series of juxtapositions and disjunctions, achieved the unexpected combination and mixing of architectural elements and scales. The spires, intended to be seen from afar, are a key component of all the churches. These spires were important urban markers. In the absence of a formally laid out city, as proposed by Wren and others after the Great Fire, they helped to present a vision of the domination of the Reformation church over the expanse of the urban topography – in much the same spirit as the axial planning and the placement of pagan obelisks acted as new symbols of the Counter-Reformation church in Rome at the end of the sixteenth century.

St Alfege, the first of Hawksmoor's churches, sits in the middle of Greenwich, south of the River Thames. The structure of the interior is relatively modest – essentially a single room – while the plan of the building is that of a cross which also incorporates the base of the tower and the east portico that faces the street. As in most of Hawksmoor's other churches, here too there is a contrast between the inside and the outside. The articulation of the massive keystones, above the windows and close to the eye of the observer, produces a jarring effect. As in many other churches, there are half windows at the base of the building, providing 'light' to what could be imagined from the outside as a sunken space of incarceration beneath the mass of the main structure.

St George's, Bloomsbury   St Mary Woolnoth   Christ Church, Spitalfields   St Luke's, Old Street

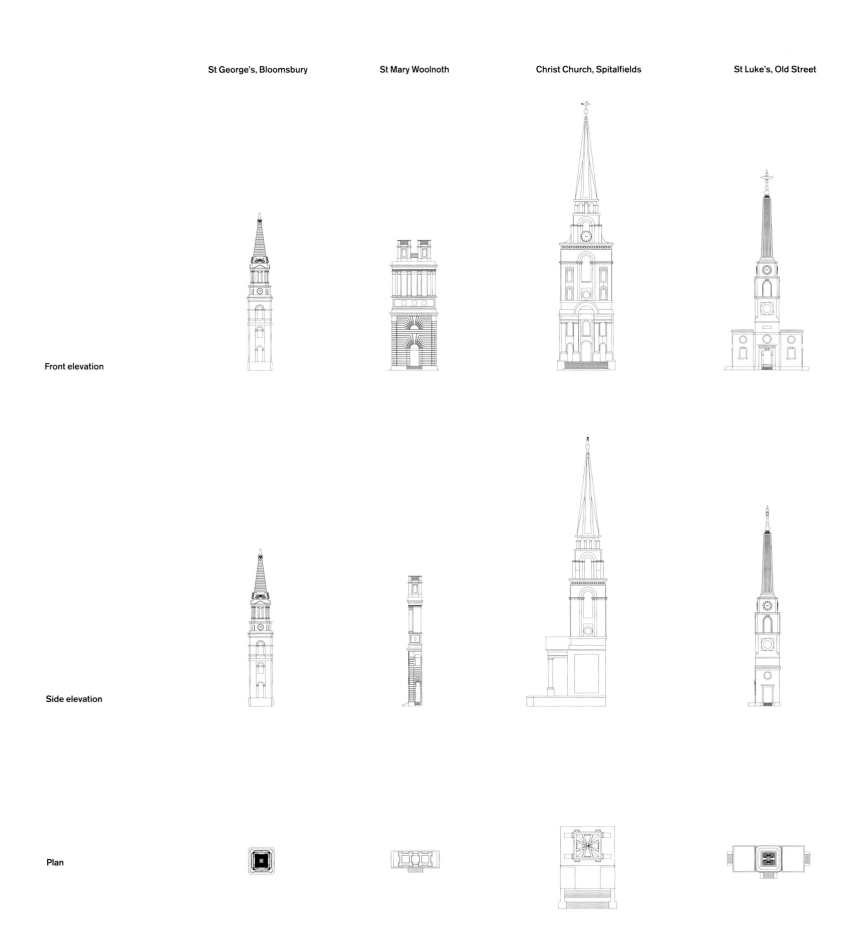

Front elevation

Side elevation

Plan

St George-in-the-East   St Anne's, Limehouse   St Alfege, Greenwich   St John Horsleydown
                                                                                              (demolished)

 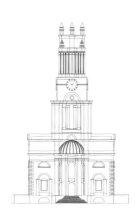  

 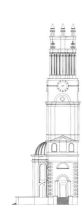  

 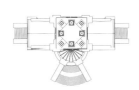

The building uses and recombines multiple architectural fragments and references: a temple front, a Roman altar, a compressed portico. At times these fragments also anticipate the utopian vision of enlightenment, and more specifically the work of French neoclassical architects of a later generation, such as Boullée and Ledoux. It was the interplay between the architectural fragments of this and other buildings and their scalar enlargement that produced the unexpected sense of awe that became so prototypical of Hawksmoor's architecture.

The reference to the ancient wonders as a source of inspiration for architecture was itself a specific form of imagining of the past. For Hawksmoor and his contemporaries there were no measured drawings of these buildings to be simply copied. Therefore his 'reimagining' of certain aspects of this architecture was primarily based on the available written descriptions of 'ancient' buildings, which became the catalysts for his own thoughts and ideas, his own projective capacities.

Apart from the literary reassessment, whether by architectural historians such as Kerry Downes and Vaughan Hart or by fiction writers such as Ackroyd and Iain Sinclair, Hawksmoor's work also assumed greater relevance when it was rediscovered in the light of an increasing interest in architecture's connection to the past during the 1970s and 1980s. In Hawksmoor, this new postmodern generation of architects saw some of its own most favoured tendencies. Although the use of irony and scalar disjunction and 'misuse' were combined with colour for the construction of an architecture that invariably lacked the subtlety and the material mass of Hawksmoor's churches, the appreciation nevertheless brought fresh attention to his work. The resulting sense of enthusiastic interest and delight makes Hawksmoor one of the most admired figures in the history of British architecture even today.

Despite the revival of both scholarly and architectural interest in the work of Hawksmoor, there has been a dearth of systematic visual and analytical material available on his work. This publication is an attempt to reveal some of the qualities that can only be seen and understood through careful study and documentation of the visual qualities of his churches.

The exteriors of many of Hawksmoor's churches have become even more awe-inspiring through the accumulation of multiple layers of dark matter on their surfaces. The consequences of age and weather have further enhanced the contrasts and the play of shade and shadow between the various architectural elements of the churches. The revealing and unfolding of this architecture could not have been achieved through mere snapshots, but had to be done methodically and with care. The black-and-white photograph had to be both an X-ray and a scalpel, capturing details and their affects through specific points of view: the unseen, the close-up, the distant and the oblique.

It is through the precision of these photographs that the churches, these methodical imaginings of the architect, are represented as architecture and as construction. You look up and see the way in which the parts of St George's, Bloomsbury come together, its various geometries resolved and juxtaposed against the columnar ziggurat of the spire rising above the building. You see how a column touches the ground, how a building turns a corner, and how the plasticity of a wall is developed.

These contemporary photographic depictions of Hawksmoor's London churches in their current state and situation are further complemented by a series of newly commissioned drawings. In their modest simplicity these drawings, plans, sections and elevations represent the churches as drawn artefacts, as measure and specification. This is, after all, what architects do.

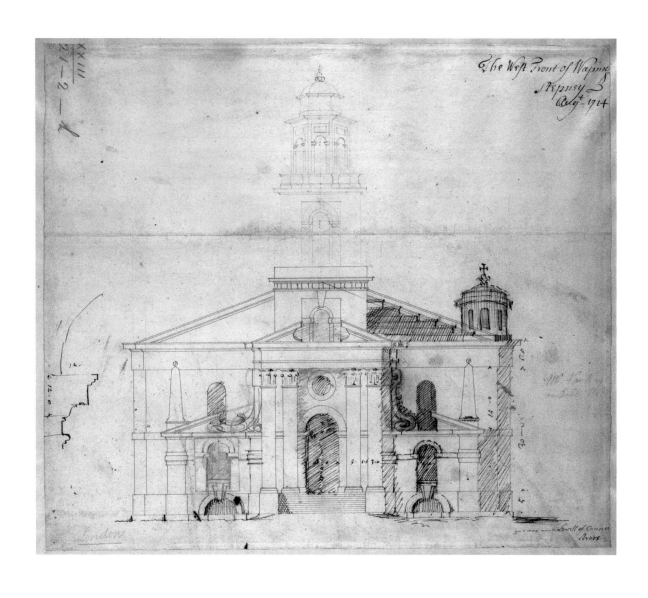

St George-in-the-East, the west front, Wapping, Stepney. Nicholas Hawksmoor, pencil and ink on paper, 1714.

Christ Church, Spitalfields, the spire. Nicholas Hawksmoor, engraving, 1717.

John Rocque's plan of the cities of London and Westminster and the borough of Southwark, showing Butcher Row in Limehouse, the River Thames and Jamaica Road in Bermondsey, Southwark. St Anne's, Limehouse is on the top right.

John Rocque's plan of the cities of London and Westminster, showing Whitechapel High Street, Spitalfields, Shoreditch and the surrounding area. Christ Church is on the bottom left.

St George's, Bloomsbury

1716–1731

Working with a comparatively small site on Bloomsbury Way in central London, without the grounds of most of his other churches, Hawksmoor concentrated his prodigious energy on the tower of St George's, which acts as a distinctive urban marker. Atop a stepped pyramid tower and wearing Roman garb, St George's namesake, King George I, looks nobly over the rooftops of London – and London looks up at him – in an arrangement based on Pliny's account of the tomb of Mausolus at Halicarnassus. Several layers of history overlap and are reinterpreted and recombined in the pyramid's textured surface. The church's Corinthian portico is echoed on each of the tower's four elevations. Reciprocally, the portico, itself modelled on the Pantheon, has as its background the off-centred tower with the porticoes and the pyramid on top. Nearby buildings, such as the British Museum, carry these playful dialogues throughout London. The interior space has generous fenestrations, which are a distinguishing feature of Hawksmoor's later churches, allowing plenty of light into the calm space inside. Renovated through a generous gift from a private benefactor, which was matched by the National Lottery, St George's has been restored to its original plan, with the congregation facing east. A meeting room in the back provides a social space after services, and a museum and yoga instructor's salon in the basement emphasise the urban nature of the space, which is open daily for visits and prayer.

0   50   100   200 m

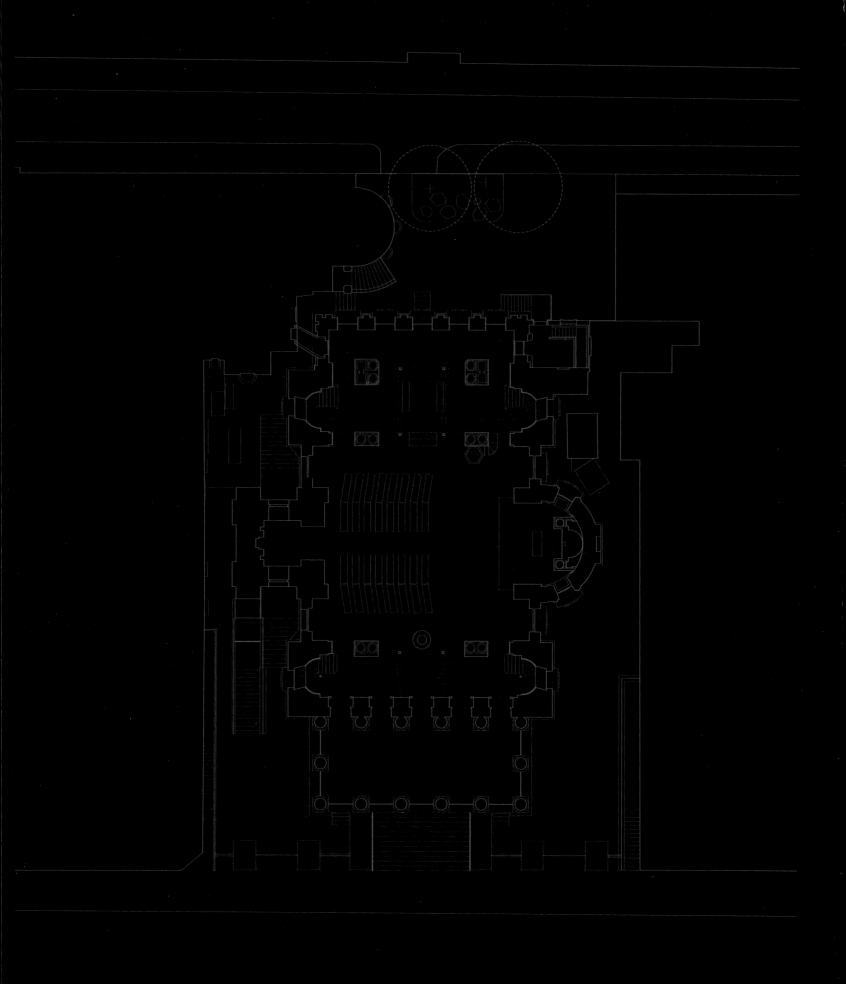

0 1   5   10 m

St Mary Woolnoth

1716–1724

St Mary Woolnoth stands at the intersection of Lombard Street and King William Street in the City of London, not far from the Bank of England. With its imposing flat façade and twin vertical towers, the building asserts its position stoically among the curves and irregularity of the nearby streets and buildings. Here, Hawksmoor plays with scale: the tops of the towers, when seen at a distance, belong to the skyline rather than to the church, suggesting the twin towers of Westminster Abbey or some other distant edifice. The church offers a place of consistent quiet and refuge amid the frantic pace of the financial world outside. Prayer services held at lunchtime on Tuesdays and Thursdays may suggest a transient banker congregation, yet the church serves a diverse population, with tourists, homeless people, and architects stopping by to see, to pray, or to be quiet. Surprisingly spacious on the inside, the plan is arranged as two squares: a smaller square supported by four groups of three columns, all enclosed within a larger square. An impressive baldaquin, with the Ten Commandments written boldly in gold lettering, calls to mind Bernini's in St Peter's in Rome. The missing galleries (removed in the nineteenth century) are somewhat disconcerting, and their absence affects the proportions. The towers remain the most distinctive feature of this church. Anyone tempted to climb to the top will pass an office space before the tower splits in two. After ascending a narrow ladder leading heavenward, one is rewarded with an unrivalled view of London.

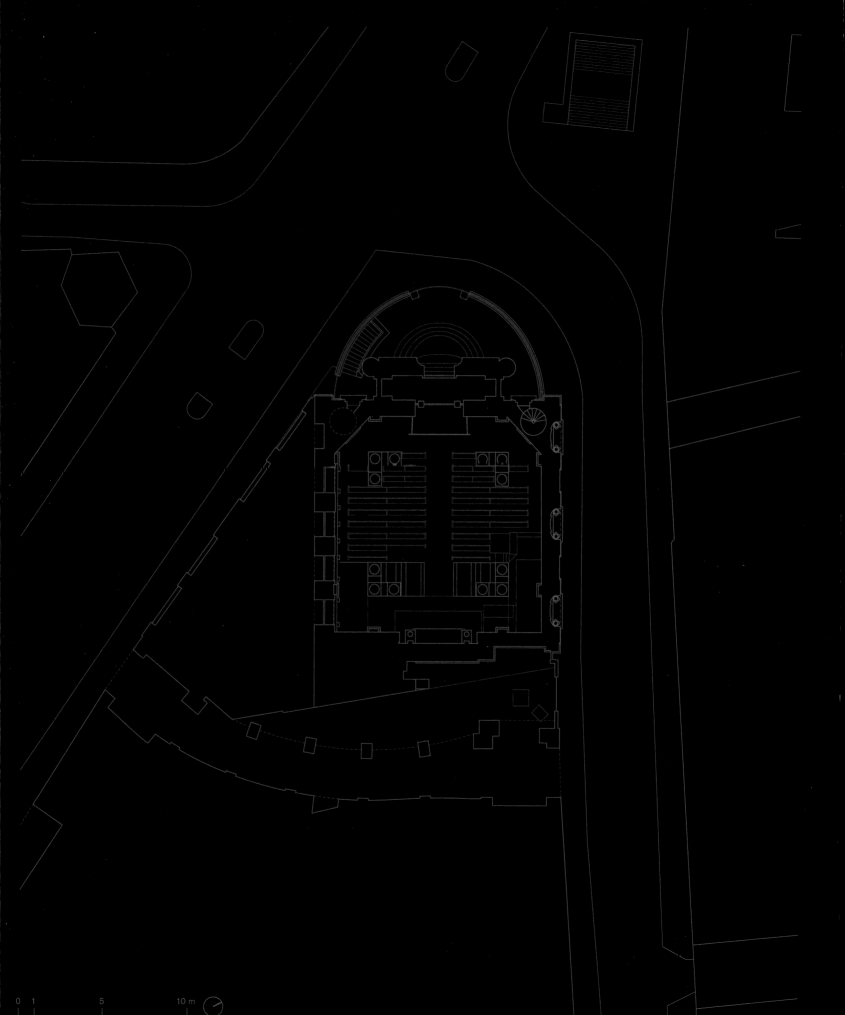

0 1   5   10 m

South-west elevation

Christ Church, Spitalfields

1714–1729

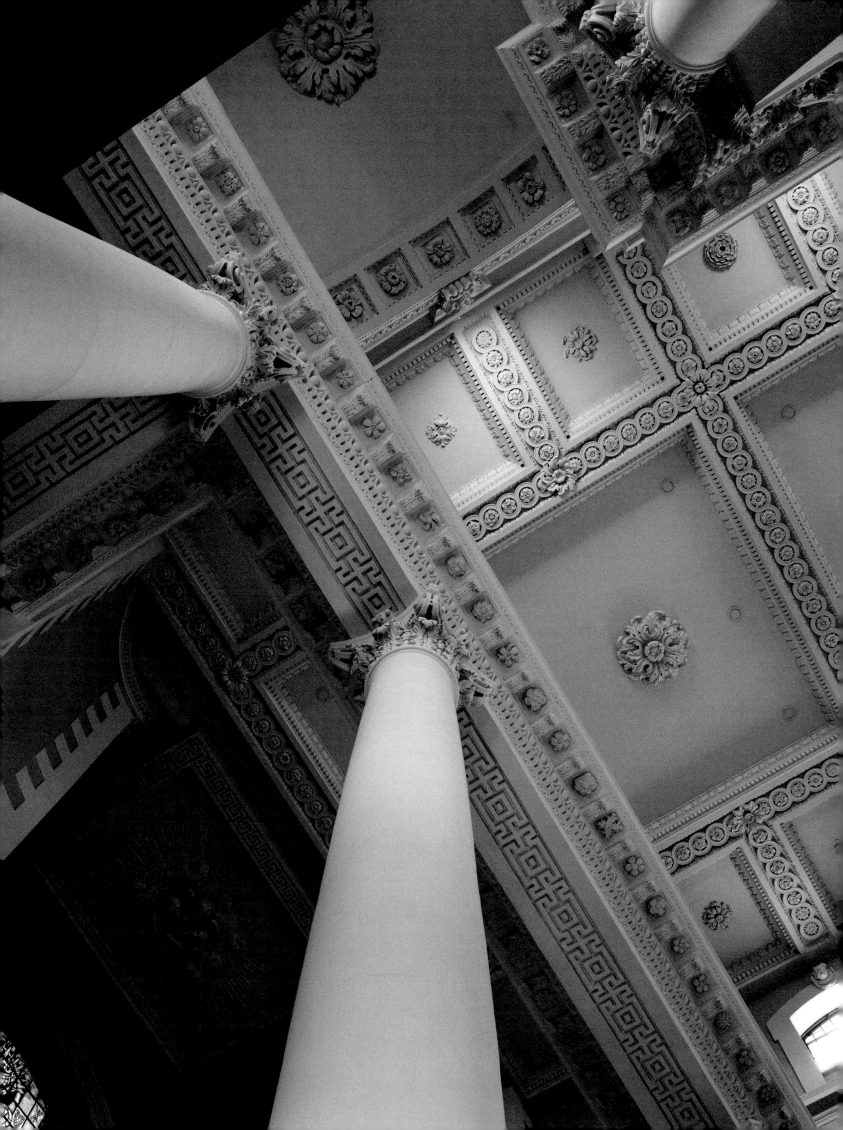

Among Hawksmoor's first commissioned churches, Christ Church, Spitalfields, with its peculiar proportions, is one of the best demonstrations of his architectural radicalism and playfulness. To this day, the white Portland stone tower is an iconic feature of the East End, a focal point at ease among the Gherkin, the Shard, and other high-rises of the contemporary city. Located on Commercial Street and forming the terminus for Brushfield Street leading from Liverpool Street Station, Christ Church holds fast among the constantly changing London neighbourhoods. The nearby Brick Lane Jamme Masjid – a former synagogue, Methodist chapel, and Huguenot chapel – sits beside the noted curry houses of Brick Lane. In contrast to the irregularity of the nearby streets and the vertical emphasis of the outside form, the interior of the church is a horizontal block of space with a richly decorated ceiling supported by a series of columns. The interior has been carefully restored to its pre-1850s state, with the altarpiece serving as the site of contemporary art installations. One significant deviation from the original plan is the seating layout, reconfigured to facilitate an evangelical congregation as well as the many visitors and worshippers who pass in and out every day, not to mention those who attend concerts that make use of the wonderful Richard Bridge organ. At once a functioning church, concert hall, and landmark, Christ Church has a reach far beyond the East End, and has become a symbol of it.

0   50   100   200 m

0 1   5   10 m

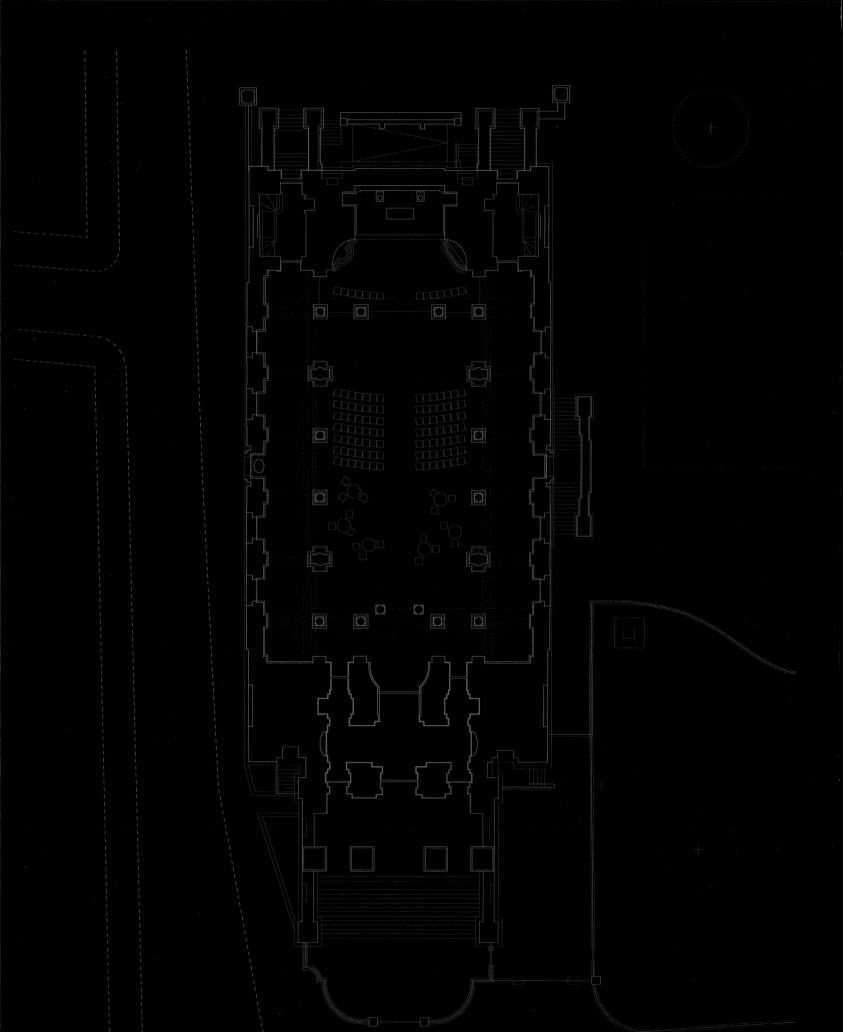

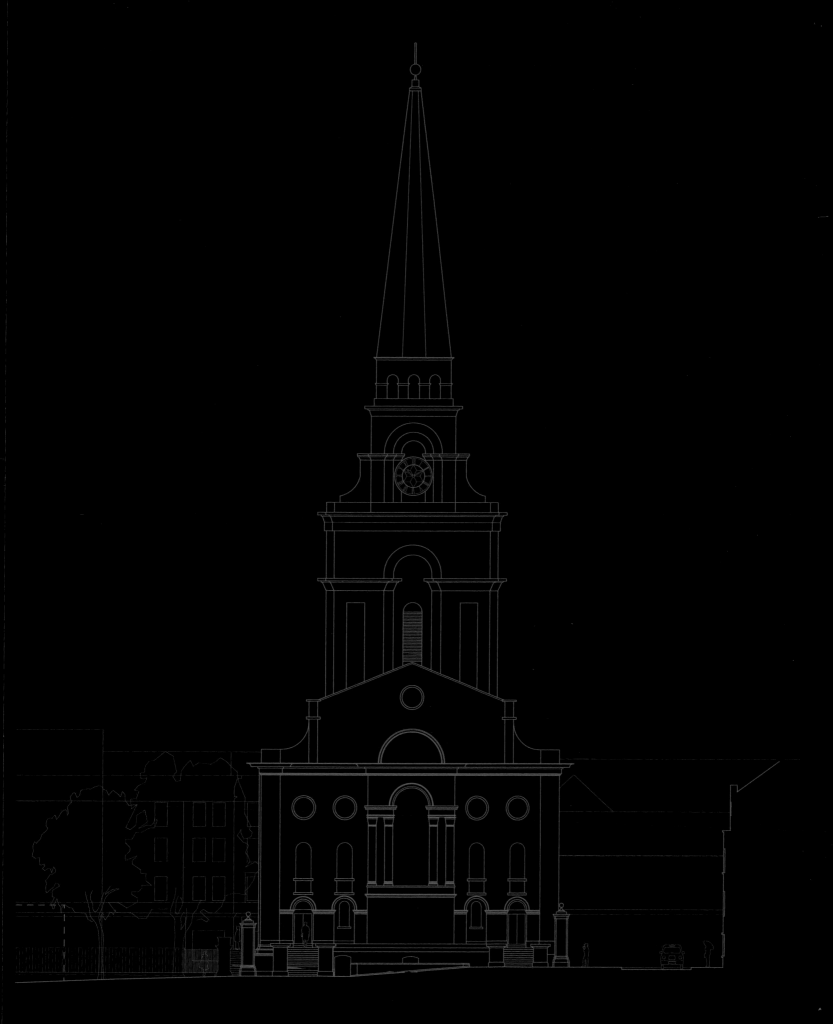

East elevation

St Luke's, Old Street

1727–1733

As one emerges from the London Underground at Old Street or takes the Old Street Roundabout from the east, the obelisk spire popping up above the treeline clearly identifies St Luke's. Not unlike the Lateran Obelisk in Rome's Piazza San Giovanni, the oddly proportioned spire and the lateral staircases were actually the only elements designed by Hawksmoor at St Luke's. The now decommissioned church was a result of collaboration between Hawksmoor and John James, who designed the body of the church. The interior has been remodelled as a concert hall and home for the London Symphony Orchestra. The churchyard has been deconsecrated and is now a park. The spire still interrupts the East London skyline as a distinctive sculptural landmark and is an assertive accent for a building now devoted to the production and playing of music.

0   50   100   200 m

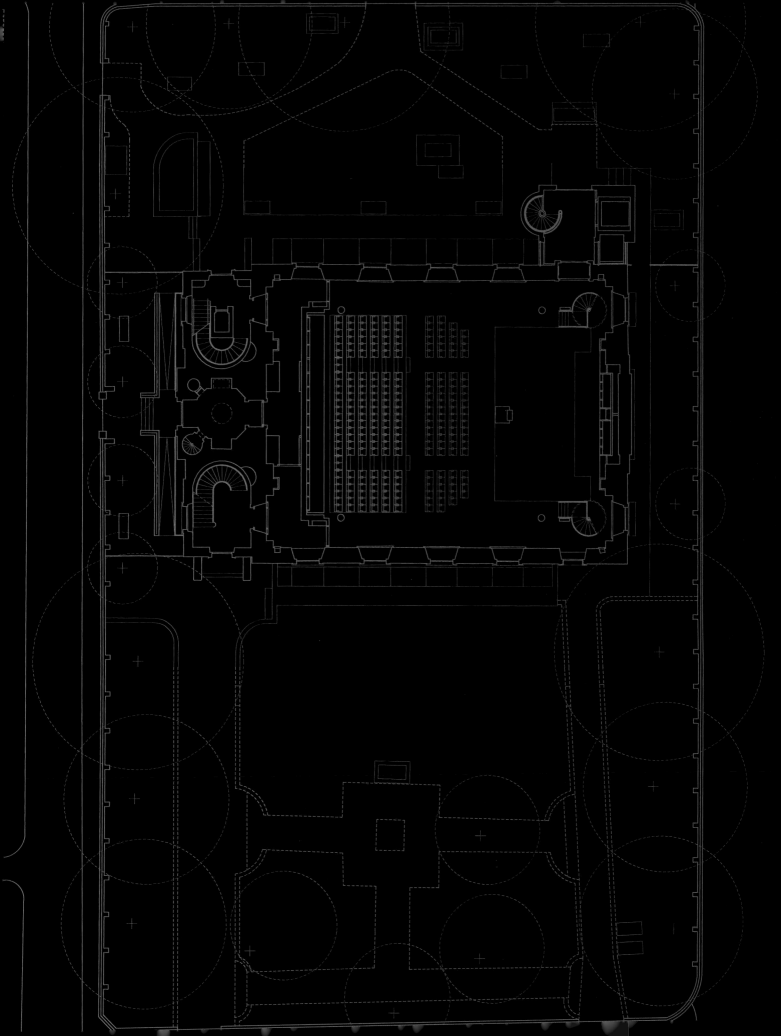

East elevation

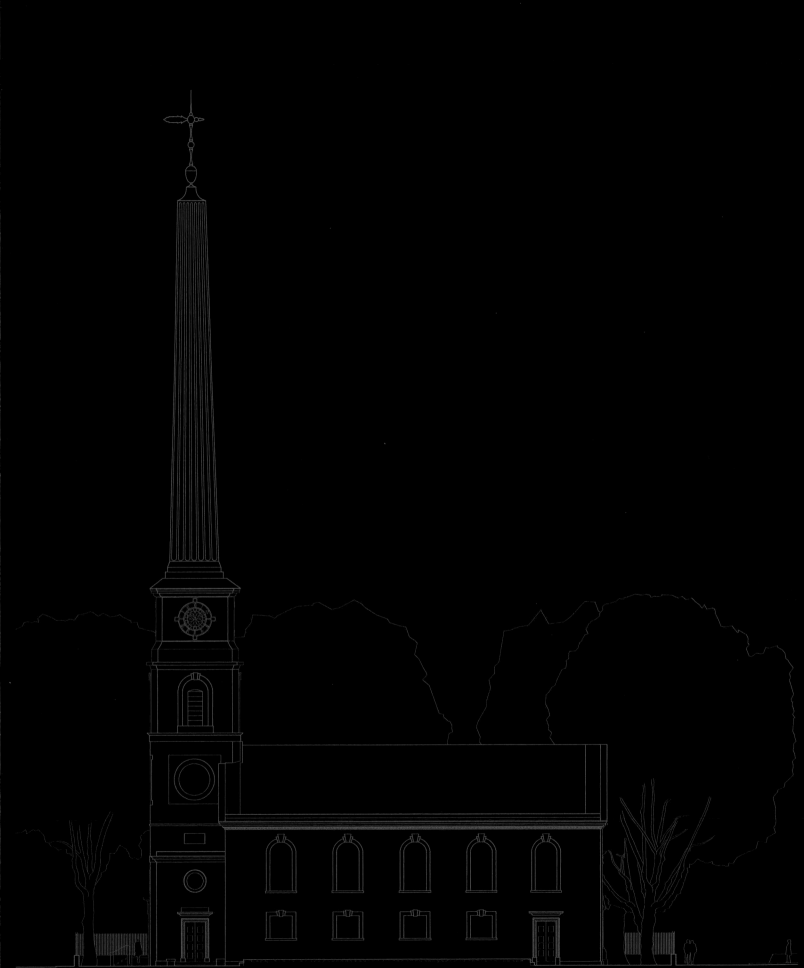

St George-in-the-East

1714–1729

St George-in-the-East lost much of its urban context during the World War II bombing of London that devastated much of the East End. Remarkably, although the interior of the church was destroyed, its shell survived the Blitz. The urban impact of the form is substantial, as the church provides a connection with a past that was largely obliterated in the war. Visible from the Docklands Light Railway as well as from the Thames, St George-in-the-East is 'a beacon of Christ's light on the Highway', according to the St George-in-the-East Prayer, and one of those urban markers that we see in passing but might not visit or necessarily know what it is. This white church has a Greek-cross plan configuring a large central space. The prominent exterior view is contrasted with a sober, almost undecorated interior space, rebuilt from the crypt level upwards after the war by Arthur Bailey. The new central space, much smaller than Hawksmoor's (and some would say better suited to the liturgy), is entered through a courtyard. Framing the interior, and yet almost totally invisible, are four dwellings neatly nestled within the former gallery spaces. These apartments are entered from the stairs leading to each of the four turrets. The play between the turrets and the main tower, and the suggestive use of these features, appeals to the senses over reason. Perhaps this connection between form and emotion – so well expressed in St George-in-the-East – is one of the reasons that Hawksmoor's work is so difficult to emulate.

0   50   100   200 m ⊕

0 1   5   10 m

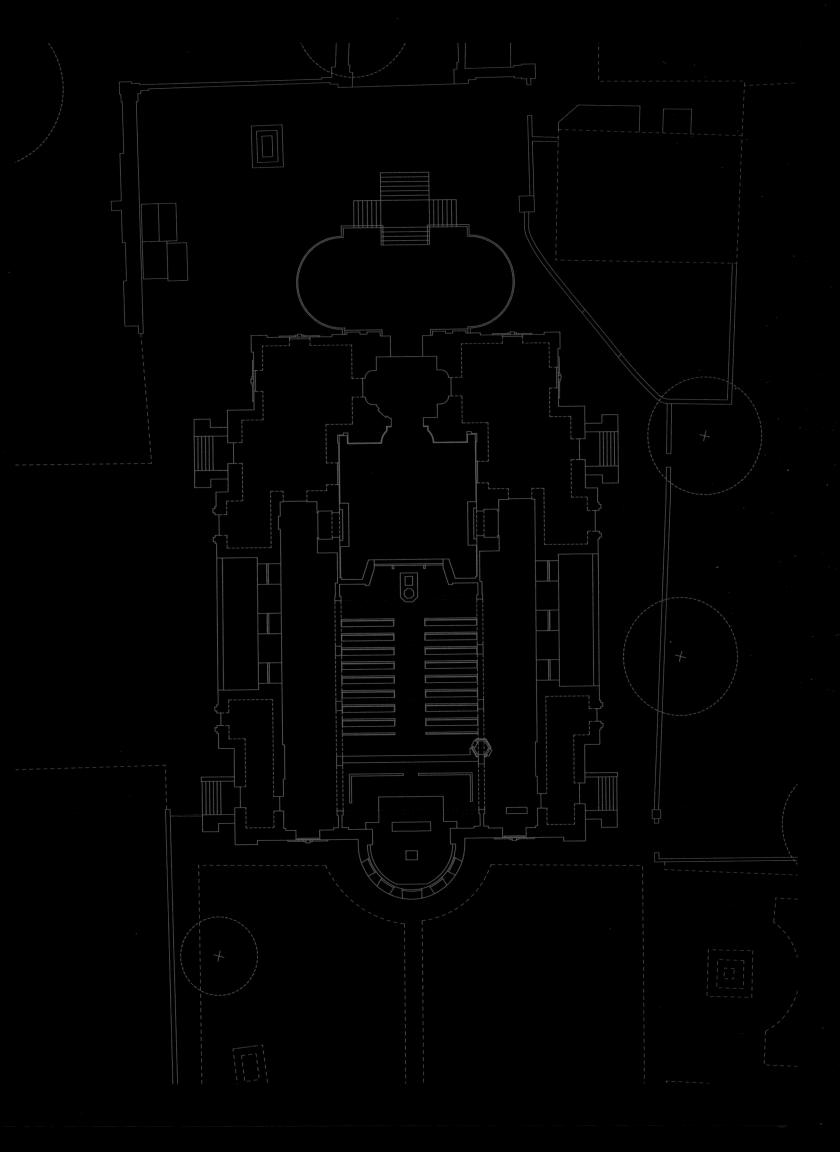

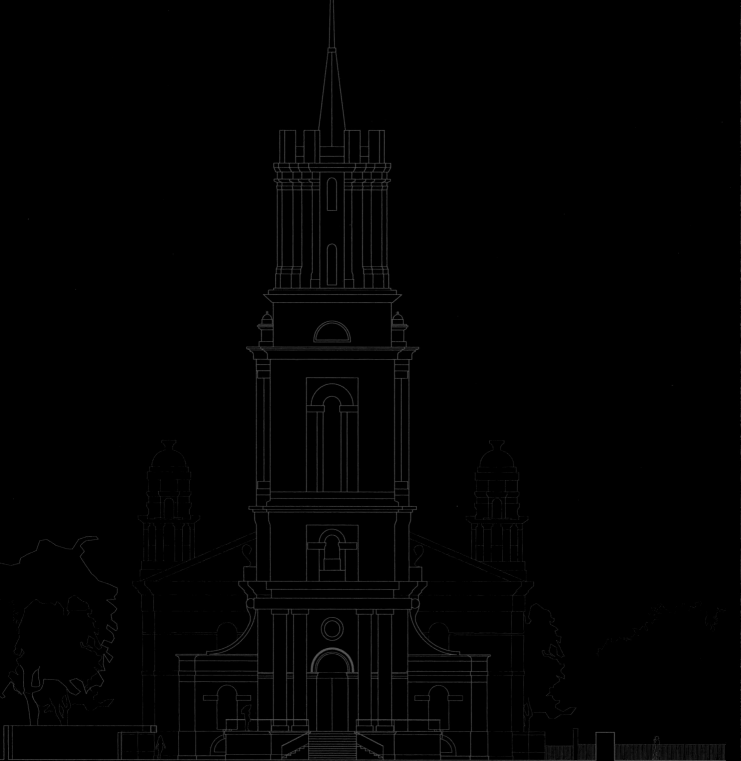

East elevation

South elevation

North elevation

St Anne's, Limehouse

1714–1730

The view of St Anne's changes radically between summer and winter. In summer, its spire peeks above the canopy of trees, but in winter, with the trees bare, St Anne's appears almost as one might have seen it in the eighteenth century. The church was designed with an imposing tower to be visible from the Thames and used in navigation – and indeed it still acts as a guide for passing ships. St Anne's is an unlikely combination of parts. Similar to Christ Church, Spitalfields, St Anne's is comprised of seemingly eclectic elements that together make a radical and distinctive whole. Hawksmoor's characteristically playful use of scale is evident in the appearance of the tower, which meets the landscape at its base with a gentle flight of steps, transitioning to a rounded entrance.

0   50   100   200 m ⊕

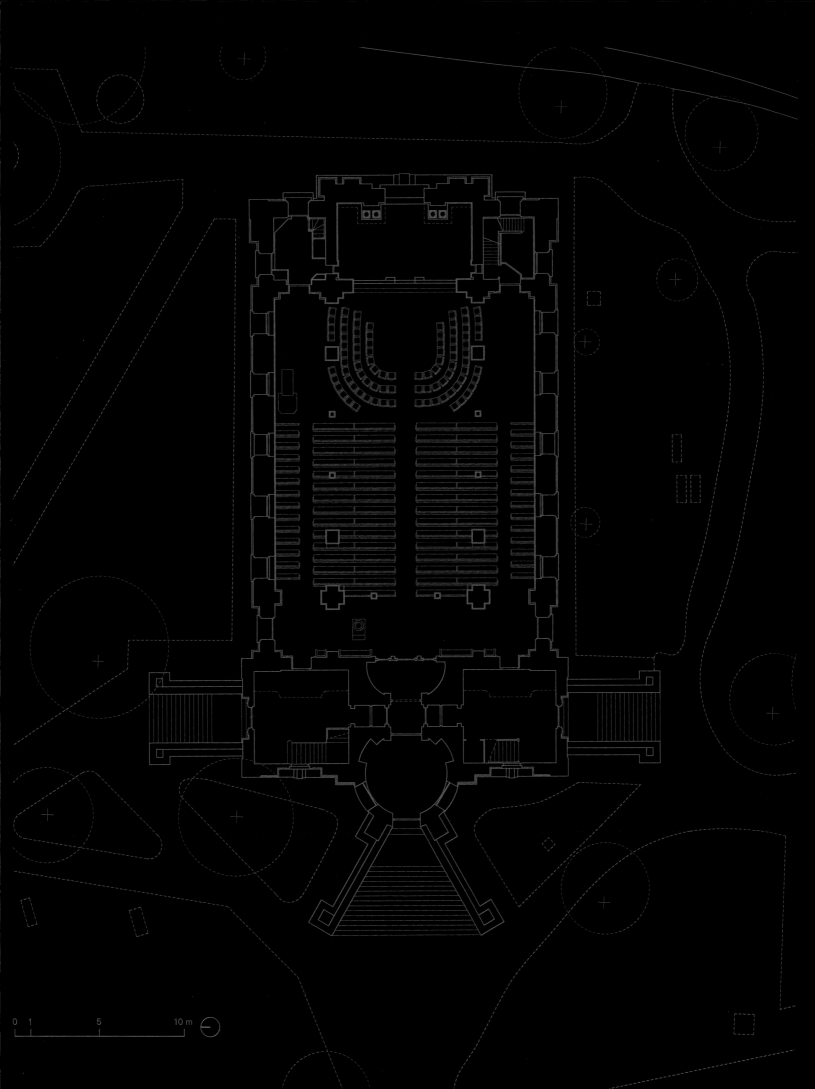

0 1   5   10 m

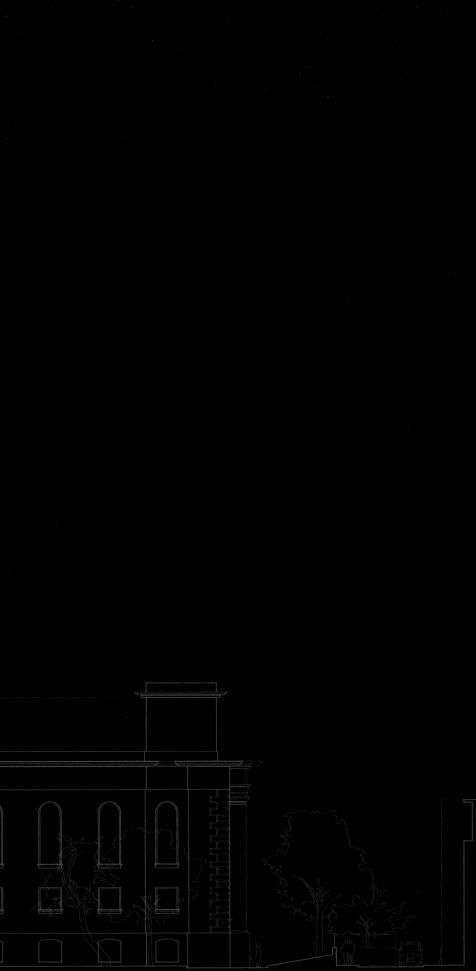

St Alfege, Greenwich

1712–1718

Located in the middle of historic Greenwich in South West London, St Alfege stands on the site of a former church where St Alfege, then Archbishop of Canterbury, was martyred in 1012. From Greenwich Church Street, the east portico is playfully aligned to give the impression of an entrance where none was intended. To the uninitiated, this portico might front a town hall, a courthouse, or a bank. The main church door is on the west, below the square steeple (remaining from the medieval structure and refaced in 1730 by John James). The tower is disassociated from the line of the street and to some extent from the church itself, yet dominates the nearby village. Whereas the east of the church is on a busy urban street, the front entrance is like a country churchyard. From the north, a narrow passage leads to the churchyard, from noise to quiet, from the city to the country. North and south entrances are used occasionally. The church is one large rectangle, with vestibules making the plan cruciform. The interior was remodelled with some unfortunate timber pairings. Nevertheless, this is one of the more complete of Hawksmoor's London churches, with a thriving congregation present not just on Sunday mornings but throughout the week.

0   50   100   200 m

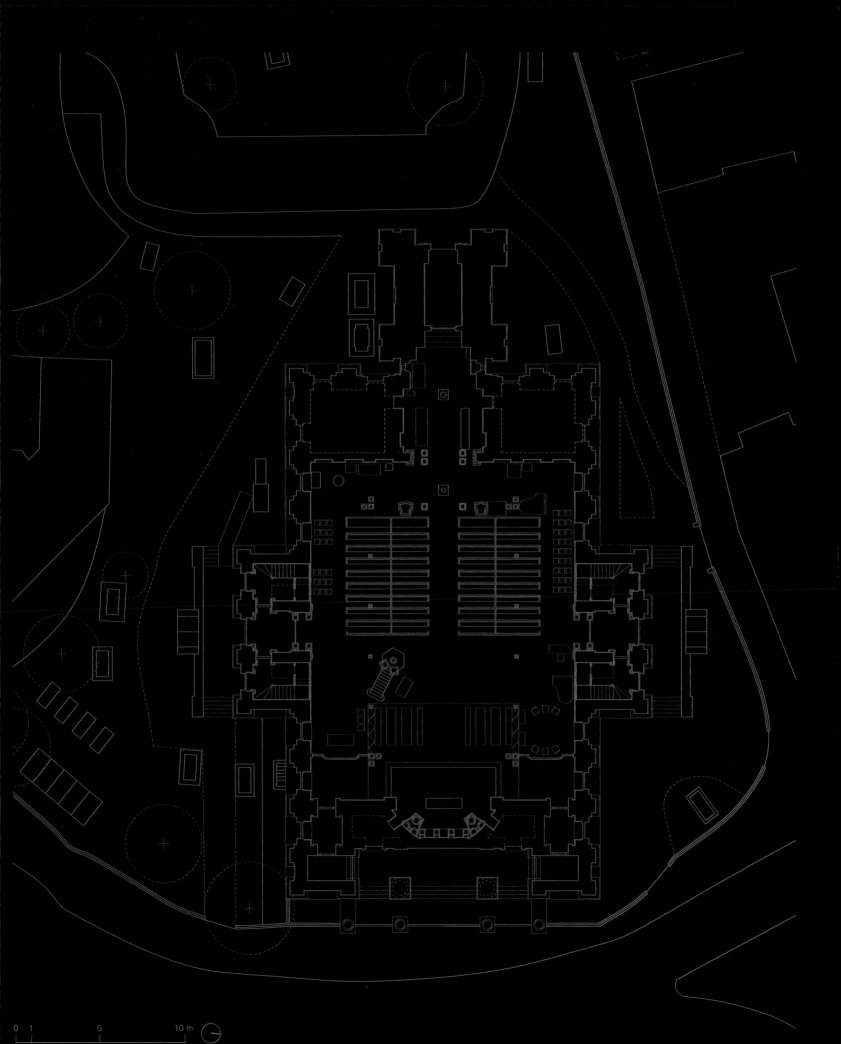

0 1   5   10 m

West elevation

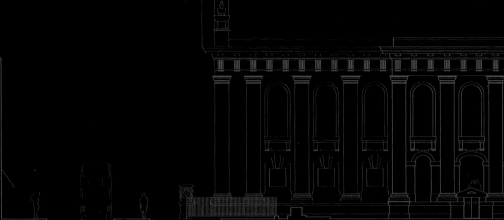

St John Horsleydown

1727–1733 (demolished)

St John Horsleydown in Bermondsey was designed in collaboration with John James. The spectacular elongated spire tapered from bottom to top, enhancing the perspective from the street. The church was bombed during the London Blitz, and today the site is occupied by the London City Mission, which conserves the base of the original building.

ST JOHN'S HORSLYDOWN.

Situate on the South Side and near the Lower End of Fair Street, from the Increase of the Inhabitants of this Part, this district was taken from St. Olaves, and formed into a distinct Parish, by the Commissioners for building 50 New Churches of which this is one, and is an Elegant Structure was finished 1732.

The present Rector the Revd. William Jarvis Abdy A.M. succeeded in 1805 the Revd. John Clark Hubbard A.M.

St John Horsleydown. Copper line engraving on paper. Engraved by William Wise (fl. 1790–1818) from an original drawing by George Sidney Shepherd (1784–1862).

Acknowledgements

This book, and the new surveys of the churches, was facilitated by a publication grant from the Graham Foundation for Advanced Studies in the Fine Arts. I would like to say a special thank you to the director, Sarah Herda. Thanks also to KPF, especially Paul Katz and James von Klemperer, for their generous support towards this publication.

I would like to thank Hélène Binet for her extraordinary photographs of Nicholas Hawksmoor's London Churches and for her collaboration. Thanks to Gareth Doherty for field research and coordination. Katrin Dielacher, Domenico Ermanno Roberti and Alastair Whiting surveyed the churches. Di Xia, Mariano Gomez Luque, Miguel Lopez Melendez, Liat Racin and Felipe Vera were helpful in compiling the final material. I appreciate Vaughan Hart's advice and friendship.

Much of the work in this book originated as part of the 2012 Venice Architecture Biennale, which also traveled to Somerset House in London in 2013. Several people made invaluable contributions to the exhibitions, including Hélène Binet's assistants, Claudia Mion, Lana Palumbo, Emilie Rousseau and Domenico Ermanno Roberti. Dan Borelli and Di Xia were responsible for the exhibition design, supported by Jane Acheson, Suneeta Gill, Theresa Lund and Lars Müller. I would like to thank Francesco Affaitato, Celia Coudert, Cecilia Puliga, Stephane Roisin, Antoine Jarrier and Davide Veneri from LOUIS VUITTON, who sponsored the original exhibition in the Venice Pavilion in collaboration with the Comune di Venezia and Madile Gambier and Renzo Dubbini. Kirstin Hay, Jonathan Powell and Stephen Doherty from Somerset House were enthusiastic supporters of the London exhibition. Thanks also to the Gabrielle Ammann Gallery, Cologne.

Jackie Brown and Chris Rawlings of the British Library kindly assisted in obtaining historic images, and Peter Inskip and Peter Jenkins Architects allowed access to their archive on St Anne's, Limehouse.

Thanks to Martina Mullis, Melissa Vaughn, and Rita Forbes, and to Lars Müller for his creative collaboration.

Last but not least, heartfelt thanks to the clergy, congregations and friends of the various churches who facilitated this book in so many ways.

MM

MOHSEN MOSTAFAVI, architect and educator, is the Dean of the Harvard Graduate School of Design and the Alexander and Victoria Wiley Professor of Design. His work focuses on modes and processes of urbanisation and on the interface between technology and aesthetics. His books include *On Weathering: The Life of Buildings in Time* (co-authored, 1993); *Delayed Space* (co-authored, 1994); *Surface Architecture* (2002); *Landscape Urbanism: A Manual for the Machinic Landscape* (2004); *Ecological Urbanism* (co-edited, 2010); *In the Life of Cities* (2012); and *Ethics of the Urban* (2015).

HÉLÈNE BINET has photographed both contemporary and historical architecture over a period of twenty-five years. Binet's work has been published in a wide range of books, and is shown in both national and international exhibitions. The first monograph entirely dedicated to her work, *Composing Space,* was published by Phaidon (London and New York) in 2012. She is the 2015 recipient of the Julius Shulman Institute Excellence in Photography Award. Hélène Binet is an advocate of analogue photography and therefore works exclusively with film.

Image credits:
Pages 2–3:
Map of London was created by Brandon Liu from OpenStreetMap.
Page 6:
Courtesy of Iain Sinclair. Originally published in Iain Sinclair, *Lud Heat and Suicide Bridge* (London: Granta Books, 2001). Map by Brian McKean from original drawings by Brian Catling.
Page 14:
© The British Library Board. King George III Topographical Collection: K.Top21 .2.h.
Page 15:
© The British Library Board. King George III Topographical Collection: K.Top23.11 .o.
Pages 16–17:
© London Metropolitan Archives, City of London.
Pages 19–165:
All photographs by Hélène Binet.
Page 179:
Published – London: J. Booth, 1814.
Originally produced for Architectura Ecclesiastica Londini; Being a Series of Views (London: Bernard Adams, 1810–1823). (London Illustrated) 129/058.

Author/concept:
Mohsen Mostafavi
Photography:
Hélène Binet
Church descriptions and field research:
Gareth Doherty
Photographic assistance:
Domenico Ermanno Roberti,
Lana Palumbo, Emilie Rousseau
Surveys and drawings:
Katrin Dielacher, Domenico Ermanno Roberti, Alastair Whiting, Di Xia
Design:
Lars Müller and Martina Mullis
Proofreading:
Rita Forbes, Pam Forbes
Scans of photographs:
Dirk Lellau
Colour separation:
NovaConcept, Berlin, Germany
Printing and binding:
Passavia, Passau, Germany
Paper:
BVS, 150 g/m²

Lars Müller Publishers
Zürich, Switzerland
www.lars-mueller-publishers.com

ISBN 978-3-03778-349-8

Printed in Germany